This journal belongs to

....

Test color

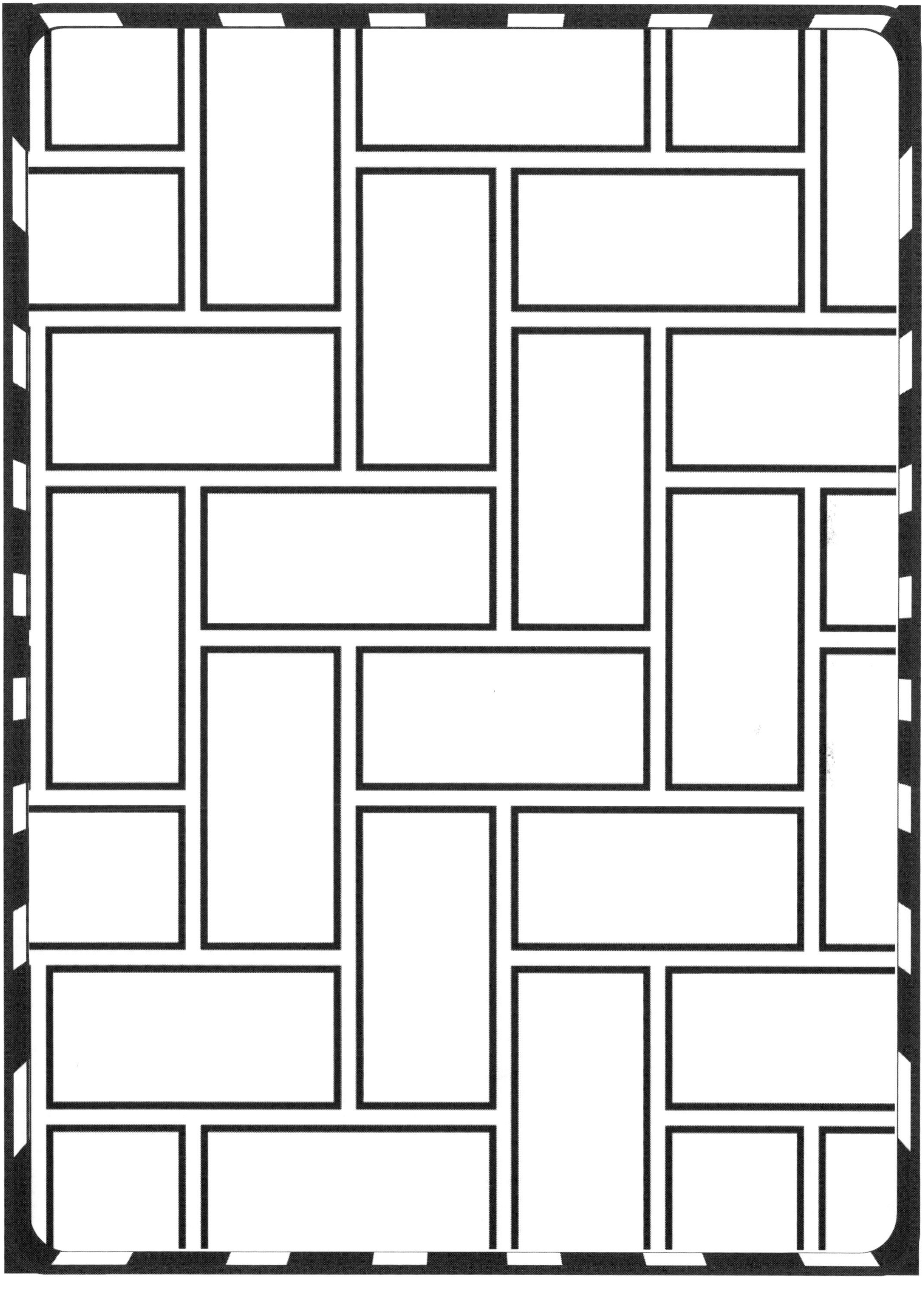

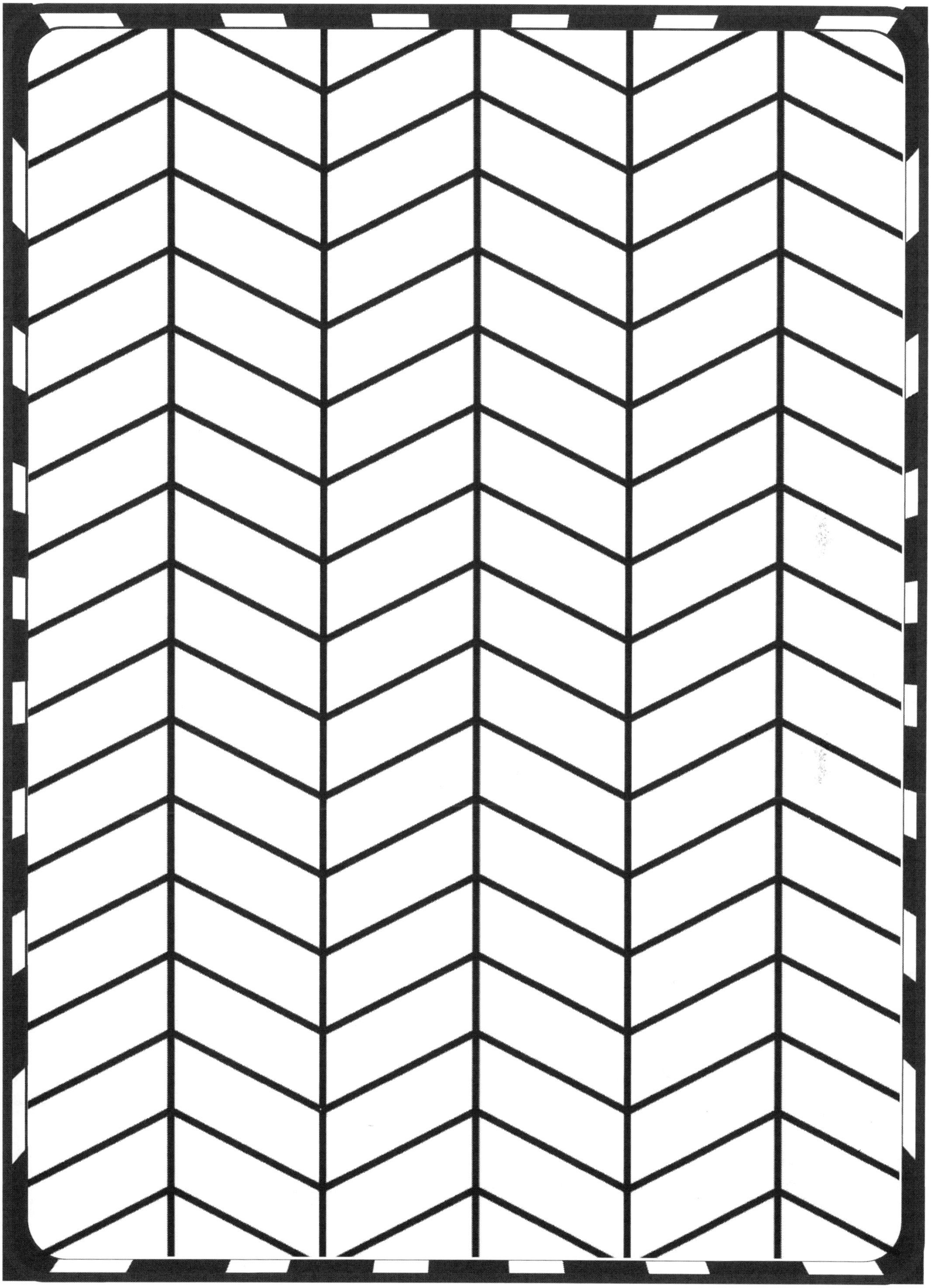

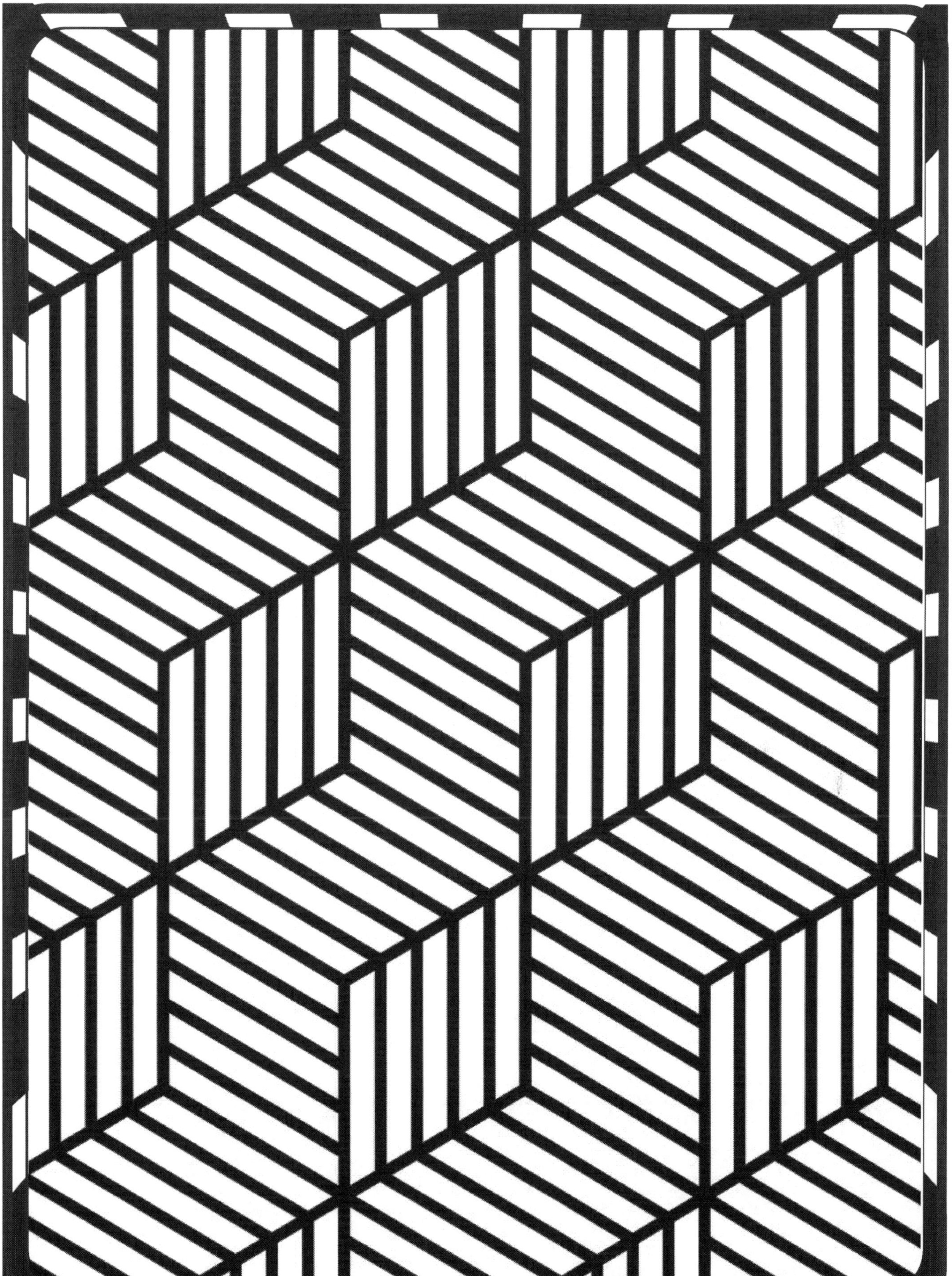

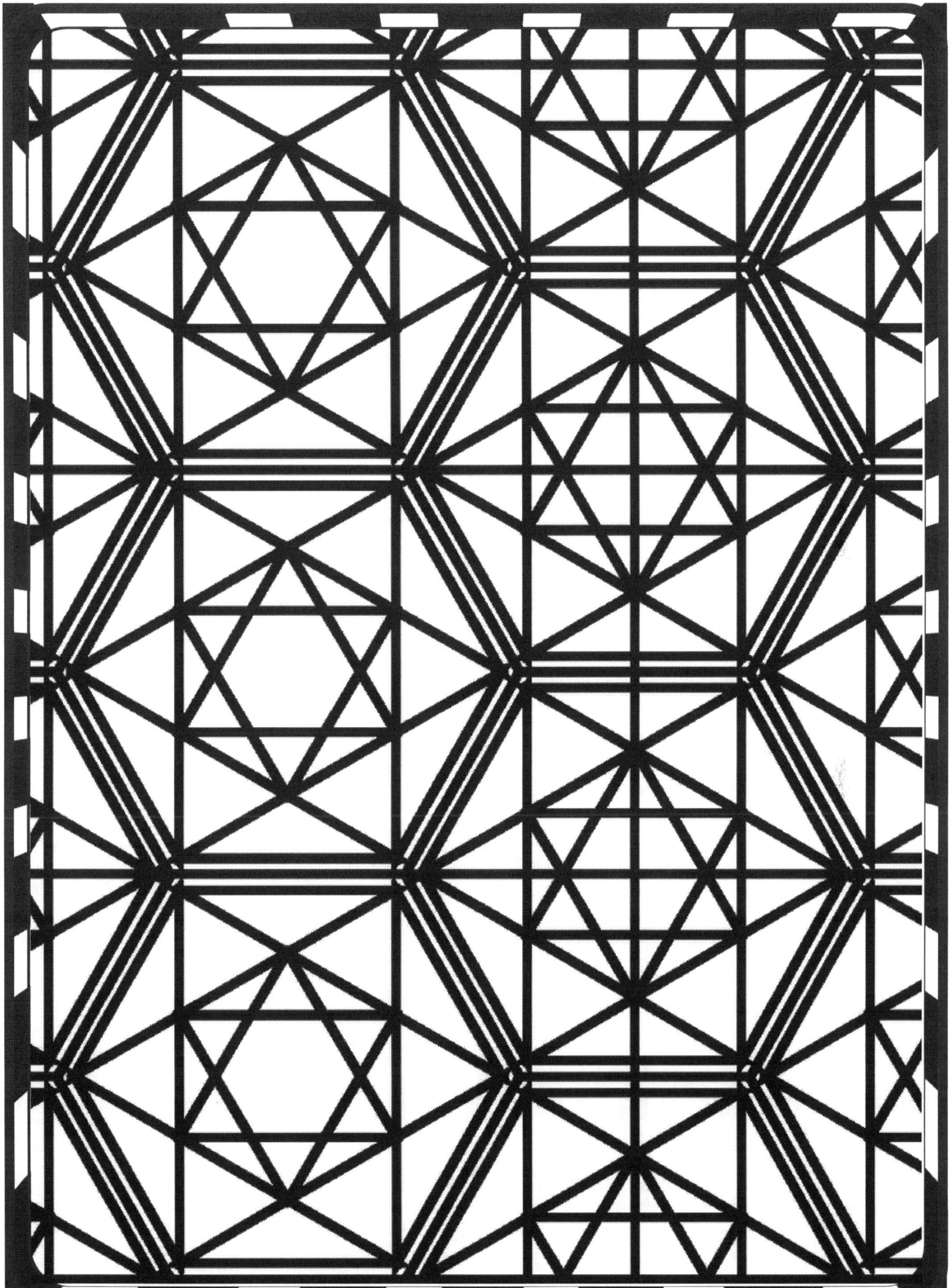

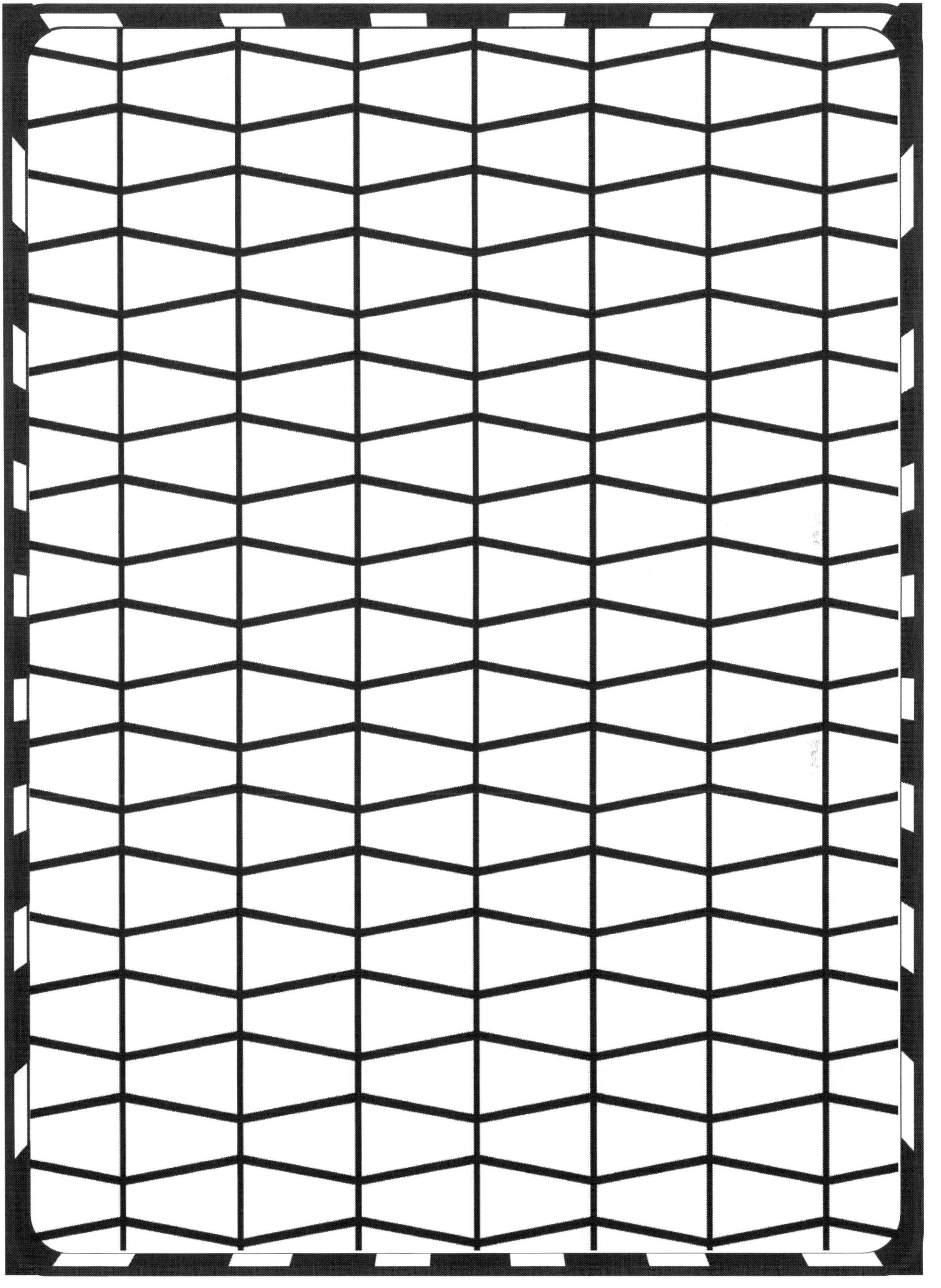

Made in United States
Troutdale, OR
09/04/2024

22594698R40073